Common Sense *for the* Healing Arts

Essays by Robert M. Duggan

7750 Montpelier Road
Laurel, Maryland 20723

Published by Tai Sophia Press
www.tai.edu

Printed in the United States of America
Book design: John C. Wilson
Cover photo: Don King/Getty Images

Library of Congress Control Number: 2003116030

ISBN 0-912381-04-3

Dedication

To my beloved Susan, for teaching me her wisdom and for loving and tending me over the past 23 years; to Grandpa Michael Whitty, who taught me the quiet wisdom of an elder; and to Tamar and Lennox, the first of my grandchildren, who remind me that it is my honor and duty to pass on through them the wisdom from my grandfather to the next generations.

Acknowledgments

THIS BOOK WOULD NOT EXIST without my collaborator of 24 years, Mary Ellen Zorbaugh. Her name belongs on the cover, and she resists. Mary Ellen came to Tai Sophia Institute to develop our first conference in 1980. She is responsible for the Institute's extraordinary publication, *Meridians,* in which these essays first appeared. This book is a collaboration—a blending of what has arisen from my work with patients and my teaching, and her ability to smooth my language in a way that results, we hope, in a gift to the reader. Mary Ellen, a profound "thank you." I want readers to be aware of the debt owed you by those who are served by this book.

A deep bow of appreciation to Phyllis Kellay, who so skillfully holds all the day-to-day strings of my work. She tends individuals and responds to calls and requests with warmth and precision, enabling me to do an often complex dance that includes teaching, administrative tasks, fund-raising, and my practice of acupuncture.

Most of what I share in this book comes from my practice—from the more than three decades of my efforts to serve individuals through acupuncture treatment. These gifts gleaned from patients come to you in the light of wisdom from the generations of my family. I think especially of my grandfather, Mike Whitty, and of the strong, firm guidance of my father, Maurice, and my stepmother, Mary. (It was my father who gave me one of the first and most significant "teaching stories" of my life. After my mother, Alice, had died giving birth to a baby sister, who also died, he said to me: "You are a very special young man. Now you have two special angels in heaven watching over you.") I also think of my sister, Patricia, and her love; of my children, Blaize and Jade; and of my grandchildren, Tamar and Lennox.

With gratitude, I acknowledge…

• Ivan Illich, my mentor for 50 years, who taught me what matters—friendship, hospitality, and service—and to question continuously what we label as "certitudes."

• Professor J. R. Worsley, who awakened me to nature's wonder and its simple rules for living. I was 33 years old when I met Professor Worsley, and it was then, through the perspective of his simple wisdom, that much of my previous learning began to fall into place.

• Friends of many years with whom I honed the gifts shared in this book in countless conversations: John Sullivan, Sherman Cohn, Anne Bartley, Julia Measures, and John Levering.

• Past and present members of the Board of Trustees of Tai Sophia Institute and the Institute's staff and faculty. I think especially of Barbara Ellrich, who has tended innumerable administrative details, freeing me to think, teach, practice, and write.

• I also honor Dianne Connelly, colleague, friend, and partner of many years and mother of my children, who has taught me to appreciate the power and nuance of language.

• My beloved wife Susan, most importantly. If I did not live my life in accord with the thoughts shared in these essays, it would be a shame—I thank Susan for keeping me on task, and for her love, warmth, dignity, commitment, and courage.

• All the members of our family. I am grateful for the richness they have brought me, particularly Blaize and Jade, and Susan's children, Suzanne and Scott.

Ultimately, it is you, the reader, who will acknowledge the wisdom and work of those named above. As you read these essays, I urge you to reflect on the wisdom you have received from your ancestors and in conversations with your famly, friends, co-workers, and teachers, and then to distill that wisdom, make it your own, and give it away to the next generations.

Table of Contents

CONTINUED

Foreword

THIS SMALL BOOK, both simple and profound, has emerged from the wisdom of a great healer, teacher, leader, and guide—Bob Duggan, who has lived in the service of healing for over three decades. We are treated to the delights of his insights on every page.

Like a well-placed acupuncture needle, *Common Sense* awakens us to healing. In these pages we see how simple healing is, after all. We share Bob's journey along the path of healing as a priest, acupuncturist, teacher, community leader, administrator, and co-creator of a healing arts school. In the tradition of *Chicken Soup for the Soul* and *Kitchen Table Wisdom,* he illuminates what he has learned in stories and observations—a bounty of wisdom. Each essay unfolds something surprising and new: how changing our perspective changes our disease; how seeing life "as it is" and "bowing to it" moves us along the path; how pain is transformed in the context of service; how embracing uncertainty and "dancing with risk" can, paradoxically, provide the certainty of peace.

Bob is not shy to point out the paradoxes of his own work: of being an acupuncturist while also stating "it's not about the needle"; of lobbying for the licensing of acupuncturists even as he warns about the dangers of professionalism; of training certifiable healers (a process that includes restrictions, standards, payment, research) while acknowledging that healing—and the training of healers—

is, at its core, beyond measurement. Yet somehow, remarkably, he shows us over and over again that grounding our intention in deep principle allows clarity to arise from paradox.

Here is a book to open at any page and let its wisdom flow over you. Here is a book to be read by all who seek to become healers of themselves or others. Common sense, yes, but with rare and uncommon revelations!

—Wayne Jonas

Wayne Jonas, MD, Director of the Samueli Institute, is former Director of the Office of Complementary and Alternative Medicine at the National Institutes of Health, and of the Medical Research Fellowship at Walter Reed Army Institute of Research.

Prologue

MY INBOX USED TO BE a major measure of my life. I thought that life couldn't really begin until the inbox was emptied and clear, until I was caught up and had things under control. Then my perspective changed. Perhaps I began to observe that no matter what I did, I was never caught up and the inbox was always refilling. Or perhaps I learned that life was about something different, about change and movement—not about getting it "right."

I write this book to share the thought that our main task as we move between our birth and our death is to learn to live peacefully day-by-day. As my wise fourth-grade teacher used to remind us, "Be at peace today, with yourself and your loved ones ... you don't know if this is the day that you, or someone you love, will die."

Living peacefully day-by-day demands common sense: eat moderately, breathe deeply, drink wisely, get plenty of sleep, accept life as it comes. And as we move through life we have a marvelous resource—our symptoms, which remind us to slow down, be peaceful, to care for ourselves. It's wondrous to me to think of the symptoms my body creates as my teachers, as *wisdom* rather than problems.

What especially keeps me going is knowing that life is about love, family, friends and community; about reaping the wisdom of the ancestors, then passing it on to our children and grandchildren. You may have read Naomi Remen's *Kitchen Table Wisdom* with its stories of healing and growing, love and death. How many of us now spend time around the kitchen table, garnering wisdom?

This collection of essays is a small attempt to pass on what I have learned in life and what I pass on to the patients I treat each day. I share it here in the hope that it will no longer be "professionalized" in the treatment room, but recovered as common, everyday wisdom—wisdom that informs our lives, that we pass on as we share meals and laughter and life with one another.

Common Sense in the Treatment Room

My Promise to Those I Serve

MY FIRST ACUPUNCTURE TEACHER in England said to me, "First you teach, then you treat, then you teach." His words made a deep and lasting impression on me. They are reflected in the words I speak to every new patient I see in the clinic. Some of these patients come in dire pain or with serious illness. To all of them I say, "My goal is to better understand all your symptoms—how they come, how they go. A further goal is to help you become an observer of these symptoms within yourself, for they are guides to living well and fully."

Symptoms are really messengers. A patient once said to me, "I never thought that asthma would be my friend." I thought referring to asthma as a friend was strange and asked, "What do you mean?" He replied, "Before I began treatment, I was frequently in and out of hospital emergency rooms, and I was taking a great deal of medication. Since I started acupuncture, I'm much more aware of the earliest moments of an asthma attack and follow these early warnings to make changes." He went on to explain, "I see that I had neglected certain things in my life—I'm aware that I'd not been eating properly, not getting to bed on time, that I'd been angry with someone in my family and hadn't cleared it. I'd been neglecting the bigger perspective, and the asthma has been a call to attention. Now I pay attention at the first sign of asthma—I look at what I've neglected in the bigger picture—and I no longer need medication."

Although not every patient has such a dramatic change, this story illustrates what is possible when we learn a new way of holding a symptom. Our body has great wisdom, and its symptoms are its way of communicating with us. Thus, I trust that a painful knee *may* be the body's way of slowing an individual in order to prevent a heart attack. I trust that each symptom has meaning and is not a random event.

I do not suggest that every symptom is understandable. I am aware that life is mystery. Many things happen that are beyond our comprehension. What I do trust is that we can learn to observe the symptoms, and—even as the symptoms come and go—we can live well and fully.

I do not promise my patients that their present symptom will go away. What I can say is that with treatment, the symptoms change and become easier to live with; and, with treatment, I am 99 percent certain that the rate of degeneration will decrease. What concerns most patients is not so much the symptom as it exists today, but the deterioration it represents and the fear of what it may become in the future. I've found that if a patient's energy is moving after four or five treatments, then almost always the deterioration slows dramatically.

Often, of course, the major symptom does go away, though not always. Those patients who experience a chronic illness frequently tell me, "I'm able to live with this now. I'm more at ease, more relaxed. I'm sleeping better." Many go on to explain, "The pain is still there, but it's not bothering me as much, and I need less medication." For these patients, the pain has receded to the background. What has happened is that the person has changed his or her relationship to the illness, shifting the focus from the symptom to being well.

How does this shift take place? Although many factors bring about this altered experience of health, it usually involves increased awareness of subtle signs from our body.

Most people, after several weeks of acupuncture treatment, report they are much more aware of little symptoms. They begin to learn this awareness during the initial examination. At this first session, I ask patients to tell me all the little things, the things they wouldn't bring to a doctor—the fact, for example, that every morning for many years they've awakened at 3:15 and gone back to sleep at 3:25. It's okay, I assure them, and explain that in the realm of Chinese medicine it has specific meaning. (This is the peak time of the Lung, the Official of Receiving, and the low time of the Bladder, the Official of Reserves.) All these little things that seem inconsequential are often pieces of a larger picture.

I also ask patients to tell me about subtle changes—how, for example, they find themselves wanting a fruit or vegetable they haven't eaten in years. This small observation can lead us to talk about their changing pattern of food cravings, and about awakening their sense of smell, hearing, and touch, so they can go to the supermarket and pick out the unique combination of foods that will nourish them. Using such little observations, patients can develop their personal design for living well.

We often hear that acupuncture is preventive medicine. I don't emphasize this aspect of acupuncture in my practice. What I do stress is "coming to life more fully" in the present. I trust that when people observe and tend themselves and have a sense of living well, this altered experience of their health will carry into the future. This is a major shift. I want to be clear that living fully in the present doesn't mean there will be no disease in the future—life is a mystery, and we must accept that mystery. We can, however, learn to live well within the cycles of life: the cycles of seasons, of day and night, and of our unique body-mind-spirit.

My goal is that my patients will understand more and more about how to keep themselves well. I want them to use me as a guide, someone to check and tend them at the change of seasons, someone to support them with the healing perspective and methods of acupuncture.

My promise is to help my patients to come to life more fully.

Winter 1993

Keep the Lid on the Rice Pot Moving...

THE CHINESE CHARACTER FOR LIFE shows a pot of rice on a fire with the lid moving up and down—a symbol of life's movement, life's constant "opening" and "closing." One way I explain my service as an acupuncturist is to say that I help "keep the lid of life moving freely." "To keep the lid moving" is closer to my goal for patients than the goal of a "healthy" life—if "healthy" means a life of continuous happiness or a life without pain and suffering.

Acupuncture is not a promise to avoid pain or sorrow or the mystery of life. It is a promise to be present to these experiences in a way that keeps life moving freely.

My goal is that my patients understand more and more about how to keep their own lives moving freely. I want them to see me as someone to check in with, who helps them tend the changes within themselves brought by the changing seasons of the year and the seasons of life itself.

I promise those I serve to ask questions that help them become better observers of themselves. How are they with particular foods or with more or less exercise? How are they when they are in love and when they are in pain? How are they when they are working hard or when on vacation? How are they when they stay up late and when they get to bed early? How are they in winter and in spring?

I do not serve my patients by making rules that they should be in bed by a certain time or eat certain foods. A mother, for example, may choose to stay up late with her sick child and then suffer the pain of a headache the following morning. What is important for her is to observe the "movement": When she stays up late and suffers a debilitating headache, at what point does she need assistance in order to continue caring for the child? When does she need to reach out into her community of friends for assistance?

Let me share with you an example from my own experience. In recent weeks my right knee has been hurting. It is not a sharp pain or a deep ache. It is more a sense of a weakness or soreness, a sense that the leg might give way if I don't tend to it. As I worked on this article, I decided to "observe" my knee. First, I noted that my discomfort was not connected to any injury. Nothing had happened to my knee. Second, I thought, "Well, I'm getting older. I could be getting 'arthritis' in my knee—it must be that kind of pain," and I considered taking aspirin or other medication. Yet, I thought how strange it was that my knee, which has been fine for 53 years, was suddenly sore.

I decided to pay attention to what my knee might be telling me before I tried to get rid of the discomfort. Could it be that this knee pain was connected to the fact that, contrary to all the rules of healthy living, I had been working too many hours, burning too many candles? In recent months, I had been choosing—and I say deliberately choosing—to push the edges of what I could do for the sake of some bigger good in the world of acupuncture, in the education of my patients, and in health-care reform in this country. I had chosen to extend myself to the point that my body was now saying, "Slow down or pay the consequences!" The lid on the rice pot, instead of moving freely, was tending to get stuck. My aching knee, an occasional headache, a different quality of sleeping, a craving for sugary foods—all spoke to me. I took two days off and rested. I went for short walks and slept and slept. Today, as I write, that knee is no longer weak. The headaches are gone, and I feel less exhausted.

I cannot say that another person's aching knee is a sign that he or she is doing too much. I do know that in paying attention to my knee—in listening to my body—I learned something about myself and made decisions that helped keep the "lid on the rice pot"

Chinese character for ch'i, the life force

Steam, or energy

The cooking rice

The Rice Pot

This "picture" of a pot of rice cooking is the ancient Chinese character for life. As the rice cooks, steam—energy, or *ch'i,* the life force—is created and moves the lid of the pot up and down.

A little bit up and down is how life is, just like the lid of the rice pot. Up and down is what we experience—and maybe going through life's ups and downs with grace is the object. Maybe that movement is what health is.

We don't want the steam so intense that it blows the lid off the pot—nor do we want it so diminished that the cover clamps down on life. We can be firmly committed to life without clinging to either our joys or our sorrows. We can learn to keep life moving, bubbling up and down.

moving up and down a bit more freely. I realized it was time for another acupuncture treatment to allow my practitioner to check my pulses and assist me in moving and balancing my life energy. I was reminded that I had ignored seasonal cycles and natural patterns of sleeping and eating and playfulness. And even though I had deliberately made these choices in order to serve what I felt was a greater good, the knee pain signaled me to observe and consider what I was doing.

To others, I offer my help in observing life and keeping it moving. In doing so, together, we will learn to live life more fully and serve life more wisely.

My promise to those I serve is to help them bear life's pain and celebrate its joy with full awareness. A colleague who had been told that he had AIDS says he has never been more alive than since the moment he confronted the reality of his death. From then on, he says, he has lived each moment fully; and he fully appreciates each person he touches. I invite my patients to such awareness, to the sweetness—sometimes the bittersweetness—of the current moment of life.

Late Summer 1993

To Dance with Risk

MY PROMISE TO MY PATIENTS is that I will be "at risk" with them.

As years go past, I am more and more aware that we dance constantly between the longing to be at risk, to be more open—more in the present, living fully—and the longing to be quiet and safe from the breathtaking, swirling movement of life.

The infant, oblivious to risk, manifests full openness—we all love to bask in the baby's glow. The teenager challenges life in ways that either take our breath away in awe or make us cringe in fear. With maturity comes the balancing act. The late summer of life brings either a centered balance, an unyielding stuckness, or great unease at not having resolved the tension between risk and security. And then in life's winter we allow ourselves—willingly or unwillingly—to pass from this dance, back into eternal oneness.

Life is movement. Illness is movement awry. My job with my patients is to facilitate movement and flow. Most of us, aware of risks of life, run to "safety," and in so doing we get stuck.

Safety, after all, is an illusion, a mirage for all who share this small ball called Earth. In truth, all of us struggle. Even so, we can have the comfort of family, friends, and community in the presence of risk and in the struggles of life's dance.

How we move in the dance makes the difference. How we open and close in the presence of another's anger, in the presence of a challenge at work, in the presence of pain resulting from an accident, in the presence of fear at the start of a new project—this determines how maturely we balance our lives and how solidly we move our feet on the earth.

My promise to my patients is that by my word, by the needle, by my willingness to be available and at risk with them, I will tend and support them in bearing up and carrying on in the face of life's difficulties.

Often I see patients who are in a dilemma—unwilling to speak the impossible word, to take the impossible step—and equally unable to decide cleanly to stay with present circumstances. They feel more and more stuck. The stuckness shows up in their body and their mind, and they feel it encroaching on their spirit.

In many cases, I've said to "stuck" patients, "Go for it! What do you have to lose?" And I've promised them (about thirty or forty people, I'd guess), "If all else fails, I guarantee you food and warmth and a bed in the basement room of my house." Susan and I wonder what we would do if, suddenly, all forty people wanted that room! The truth is, that supported by my willingness to be at personal risk with them, patients do find the courage and will to move on. Thus far, the room remains empty.

I have had the gift of experiencing more personal risk than most: the risk of practicing acupuncture when it was almost unheard of in the USA; the risk, with others, of opening this Institute; the risk of publishing *Meridians*. Then there is the risk of truly listening to my children (no matter what the story); the everyday risks of driving a car; of getting up in the morning! I know I am blessed, and I share this with my patients, those I serve.

Spring 1994

Seasons and Symptoms — Our Teachers about Life

RECENTLY I WATCHED A MAN—I'll call him Greg—receive acknowledgment from about forty people for whom he had done extraordinary work. While the group gave him resounding applause, Greg stood with his head bowed, his shoulders rounded, his hands in front of him. He appeared to merely suffer the acknowledgment. As the applause ended, he smiled weakly and said "Thank you" in a shy voice. Later, I was told that Greg used an inhaler for chronic bronchial problems, and that he often felt insecure about his work, doubting his ability to make a contribution to others. In conversations with him about projects for which we shared responsibility, I observed that he found it hard to let go of a topic or to conclude a discussion.

As I reflected on these "symptoms," I thought, "Wouldn't it be wonderful if he could throw back his shoulders, open his chest, look at people as they gave him applause, and take in their gratitude and respect? Wouldn't it be marvelous if he could experience *inspiration*—the in-taking of breath that would fill his lungs and spirit?"

I wondered if he knew that in Chinese physiology his emotional and physical symptoms are related? In Chinese medicine, the lungs and the breath are connected with the ability to take in, to receive—they are aspects of the Metal element, associated with the season of Autumn.

The Metal element also includes the colon and the ability to let go and end things. What if Greg understood that his difficulty in ending conversations and his closing out of applause were related? That his insecurity and lack of awareness of his own power were linked to the rounded shoulders which almost shut off his lungs, to his downcast eyes and low voice, to the inhaler and the bronchial condition?

Greg makes a major contribution to many people. He has good reason to take in their acknowledgment, to draw deep breaths. He senses the needs of others wonderfully. What would it mean to others, I wondered, if he gave them a further gift—the gift of receiving their acknowledgment.

If Greg could see the pattern in these phenomena, I thought, he would begin to make changes, to live a fuller life.

As I work with the people who come to me for acupuncture treatment, they begin to see how various facets of their lives interact and relate. I try to teach this awareness by word, by suggesting a reading, by encouraging them to come to a seminar. They begin to see how various facets of their lives interact and relate.

So here, with the hope that more and more people will understand ways in which we can come to life more fully, I will point to some of these relationships. Looking at our daily lives through the eyes of Chinese medicine, we'll travel around the cycle of the five Elements and the cycle of seasons.

Autumn and the Metal Element:

Issues of Letting Go and Letting In

In describing Greg's situation, I've described the correlated phenomena of the Metal element and the Autumn, the time when life has reached its fullness. In nature's cycle, this is the season of letting go: Earth lets go of Late Summer's rich harvest; trees let go of their leaves; nature lets go into Winter. For us, too, it is time for letting go, time for acknowledgment of the year's work and for taking a deep breath in awe of the magnificence of life. The Metal phase (think of gold and silver) has to do with the way quality, respect, inspiration and awe show up in our lives.

In Greg's story, we saw that issues such as self-doubt and holding on too long link with our physical selves: our lungs, our bowels, the way we open the chest and take in deep breaths.

Winter and the Water Element:
Issues of Fear and Power

As we move from Autumn into Winter, we enter the deep cold, the deep mystery, the deep power of nature's cycle.

In Chinese medicine, our bodily fluids hold our deep reserves. The Kidney, the organ associated with the Winter/Water phase, is like a battery, generating power as it generates urine. When all goes well with our Water element, we have a sense of deep-down power. Profound exhaustion may signal that our Water is out of balance. A related yet opposite sign is having too much fluid—we may retain water, almost drowning in our bodily fluids. Chinese medicine teaches us to look for such opposites: Where there is great power, there is also danger of too much pressure.

Other opposites "dance" in the phase of Winter/Water: having power and fear of claiming our power. (Fear is the characteristic emotion of the Water element.) We may say, "I can't go on with things because I'm too afraid." Yet fear actually generates power. Celebrated actor Sir Lawrence Olivier once said that he never wanted to go on stage *without* stage fright. When we understand that where there is fear, the full power of life is present, then we can feel the fear *and* get on with life.

Sometimes, however, we respond to fear by plunging ahead too soon. We may be so afraid of remaining in the unknown that we act prematurely, before we've drawn sufficiently on the wisdom that can emerge from the deep Waters. So we try to escape our fear by moving too soon into action, into the Springtime of the cycle.

Spring and the Wood Element:
Issues of Anger and Blocked Life Force

Nature's energy thrusts upward in the Spring. Buds burst through woody stems; plants push through the earth. For us, too, the Springtime brings new energies, new beginnings, and visions of the future. This is the creative phase of the cycle. The organs associated with this phase support our creativity and rising energy: The Liver provides all its creative chemical interactions, and the Gall Bladder, with an energy pathway extending from eyes to toes, brings an encompassing 360-degree perspective on life.

When our Spring/Wood energy is out of balance (either too

aggressive or weak, for example), we may be unable to begin new enterprises. Or we may hear ourselves and others speak in a shouting, angry voice. The shout comes when our rising energy is blocked. On hearing the shout and observing the anger, rather than responding with frustration, we can think, "I wonder how the force of life is blocked?" We can ask the same question when we hear ourselves or others speaking in weak or mumbling tones. Sometimes these imbalances arise because we haven't stored within ourselves sufficient self-respect and inspiration from the Autumn/Metal phase, or power from the Winter/Water.

Summer and the Fire Element:

Issues of Joy and Intimacy

What we initiate with the thrusting, creative energy of Spring unfolds in the summertime, the phase of warmth and joy—a joy that comes after the hard work of Spring: creating a vision of the future, making breakthroughs, starting something new. Joy, intimacy, and playfulness are the gifts of the season of Fire.

All the great wisdom traditions concur with the Navahos who say that our visions and actions should serve our children's children and honor our parents' parents. In the Summer/Fire phase we attend to our generational relationships "up close and personal." For many, it is the time of family visits and renewal of friendships. When the energy of Fire flows freely, it draws us together in intimacy and playfulness.

More broadly, Summer calls us to look at the presence of joy and intimacy in our life: Do we have too little joy? Excess joy? Appropriate joy? Do we have appropriate intimacy? Many points on the Fire meridians (which include the Heart, Small Intestine, and Circulation pathways) have to do with openness, intimacy, and vulnerability. Acupuncturists can use these points to help stimulate or calm the warm energy of Summer/Fire.

Late Summer and the Earth Element:

Issues of Appreciation and Thoughtfulness

When Fire reaches its peak, its energy begins to wane into Late Summer, the time when we harvest the fruits of life. This is the phase of the Stomach and Spleen, of sugar metabolism, of the ability to digest and process. This is the season to savor the sweetness of life, to be thoughtful about what we have received and accomplished—not to indulge in endless ruminating or worrying or cloying sweetness (symptoms of Earth energy gone awry). In this energy we nurture others, helping them, too, take in their personal harvests. So in Late Summer we accept life's rich harvest, use it thoughtfully, and store it away for the Autumn and the Winter. When the Late Summer phase reaches its fullness, we begin to move on into Autumn's inspiration and respect.

Opening Fully to Life

We can quickly examine the energies within ourselves at the physical level: *Autumn/Metal:* Are we able to breathe deeply and have good bowel movements? *Winter/Water:* Does our urine flow appropriately—not too much, not too little? Do we have appropriate thirst? Do we have adequate energy reserve? *Spring/Wood:* Can we sleep at night? *Summer/Fire:* Do we sweat appropriately when it's hot? *Late Summer/Earth:* Do we enjoy our food and have a hearty appetite? Is our weight stable? If we can say yes to these questions, we know that we are doing well; we know our body is functioning appropriately in all five energies.

Similarly, at another level, we can ask if our daily activities include a mix of joy and intimacy and caretaking, of grieving and the pains of life, of fearful respect for the power in life, of joyous vision and creativity. If we live in all those energies, then we are well.

Look at the small child who so unselfconsciously cycles through all the phases, often within a few moments: She longs to be held and taken care of, then bursts into excitement and activity; she laughs, then saddens at the loss of a toy. We know the child is well when she can cycle quickly through these emotions. If the child seemed stuck in a phase, however, never exhibiting some one of these emotions, we would be concerned.

It is the same with ourselves: Do we experience the full cycle of emotions and passions? Do we open ourselves fully to life?

Winter 1994

Tending the Rice Pot

IT'S A WONDERFUL METAPHOR FOR LIFE — the Chinese character that depicts rice boiling in a pot, its lid bouncing up and down to represent life's up-and-down movement. Let's return to that image for another lesson about living life well and fully.

When life is going well, it is moving up and down. When life is stuck, the pot's not boiling and the lid isn't moving. When we are fully alive, the lid is perking. We've all had the experience that sometimes life gets stuck, and sometimes the lid seems to blow off, and sometimes it goes along at a steady rate. That steady, up-and-down rhythm of life includes suffering and change as well as the good times. There's no avoiding it.

Environmentalists remind us that everything is interconnected. In health care, however, we've focused principally on one part of the interconnected whole: We've concentrated on the form of care that deals with pathology—care that acts best when the lid is stuck or when the lid has blown off.

Chinese medicine teaches us to observe the whole—to notice the little "glitches" in life's movement and tend them before they reach the pathological stage.

My patients sometimes come in saying, "Well, I'm fine. I'm just here for a preventive checkup." That is never the "truth." Always some signs or symptoms are speaking. The body is always putting out a sign that concerns the patient. Yet people feel it's not legitimate to speak of it because it has not yet become a pathology. They sense the signs but don't know how to read them.

Each of our adverse symptoms is a movement, known or unknown, that offers us the possibility of learning to live the up-and-down rhythm of life. When individuals fight that rhythm, they are more likely to develop a pathology. When they learn to understand and live in the rhythm, they are more likely to function well. Elderly patients, for example, may learn to see their arthritic pain as the symptom that slows them down and prevents a deeper distress. In this way my patients begin to see themselves in charge of their life rhythm. They learn that they can keep it going.

I spend much of my clinical time reestablishing that power in the patient. Individuals whose symptoms heal quickly, who go away appearing to be cured by the needles, often go away before they experience this process of opening and closing and opening and closing—before they become aware of their own ability to control the process. Those individuals often return, treating me as if I were a mechanic responsible for fixing their problem.

As the needles of acupuncture make the life force more responsive, they help people become more aware of small signs—signs that precede the more obvious symptoms. Perhaps a stiffness or a tiredness that comes before arthritic pain—a signal to slow down without waiting for the pain. These small signs are guideposts to personal responsibility.

The late Norman Cousins wrote in *Time* about our ignorance of these signs and our failure to take responsibility for our health: "We are becoming a nation of weaklings and hypochondriacs, a self-medicating society incapable of distinguishing between casual, everyday symptoms and those that require professional attention.... We fail to learn that pain is the body's way of informing the mind that we are doing something wrong."

Cousins goes on to say that we need to be reeducated about our health, and develop confidence in our ability to care for ourselves. "We can have greater confidence in the reality of a healing system that is beautifully designed to meet most of its own problems," he says. "And even when outside help is required, our own resources have something of value to offer in a combined strategy of healing."*

That is the reality that I, the health practitioner—the farmer tending the elements of an individual's movement—must deal with. In coping with the wind, the rain, the texture of the soil, the effect of chemicals, and so on, the farmer must constantly attune himself, learning the rhythm and movement of the area in which he is working. It's my goal that patients, too, attune to their own energy and learn to "farm" themselves.

I ask you to observe your own movement in this moment. Are you up, down, stuck, anxious? Are you judging, listening, absorbing, receiving, sorting? Are you open or closed? Does that movement serve you, or is it an old pattern? Does that pattern open you to life more fully? Simply observe yourself. There is no judgment. The observation of what *is* makes possible new movement.

With new movement, with awareness, we can keep the lid on the rice pot going up and down. We can come to life more fully.

* Norman Cousins. *Time,* June 18, 1990.

Simple Ways to Tend Ourselves that Make a Big Difference

I remind people who come for acupuncture about the simple things we can do to care for ourselves—things that make a big difference in our well-being.

SLEEP. So often people complain about a symptom, and, when asked, report that it doesn't occur if they get enough sleep. They're surprised when they make the connection between sleep and symptom. Sleep is one of nature's best treatments, and it's inexpensive and noninvasive. The body prefers to follow the natural cycles of day and night, so eight hours of sleep between 11 p.m. and 7 a.m. may be more beneficial than the hours between 12:30 and 8:30. If you get very busy and are not sleeping regularly, ask yourself if the activity is worth the cost of your symptoms. Does your activity serve the community—tending sick relatives, for example, or working on a project that benefits many?

WATER. Do you drink enough water? It helps generate our chi, our life energy. Keep a cup of water on your desk and sip frequently throughout the day. Often we think we're hungry when we're simply thirsty.

AIR. Breathe deeply. When we get busy or upset, our breathing becomes shallow. Stop and take a deep breath; don't speak until your breathing has settled. Breathing in his way helps us recover our internal "observer"—our ability to see life clearly.

MOVEMENT/EXERCISE. No big deal—just simple movement. Begin with twenty minutes of brisk walking three times a week. The regular practice of yoga, tai chi, or qigong builds helpful patterns of breathing and exercise.

FOOD. Eat plain, good food at regular times. Sometimes symptoms are the body complaining that it doesn't get regular nourishment. The Chinese saw the body as Twelve Officials. A symptom simply may be the Officials complaining that they don't know when they will be fed next.

CLEARING OUR UPSETS. When we hold onto upset in our thoughts, our bodies hold it, as well. A good policy when upset: take a deep breath, then honestly take steps to change the situation—or let our upset go.

These simple basics work for me. I offer them to you.

Autumn 1996

Common Sense
at Home, at Work, in Society

Living with Paradox

I HAVE WRITTEN AND SPOKEN FREQUENTLY about the importance of being an observer, of seeing life exactly as it is and then bowing to it, accepting life fully, just as it is. The Tao, the Oneness of life, calls us to accept life, to live in the presence of life living us. It affirms that life is perfectly okay just as we find it.

Someone who knows me might read that and say, "Duggan, you don't practice what you preach. You didn't bow to life exactly as you found it when you moved to Maryland in 1972. You and your colleagues worked to create the Institute and to change the course of medical practice in Maryland. That wasn't 'accepting life as it is.' And those groups from the Institute that are working in Baltimore prisons, hoping to break the cycle of prison-release-crime-early-death—they aren't bowing to 'what is.' Furthermore, when you and other acupuncturists treat persons coming to you with pain and suffering, and these people leave happier, often without the suffering—that's change! As a practitioner you aren't just bowing to life as it is. So which is it? Bow or change?"

It's both.

The great 16th-century Christian mystic, John of the Cross, who deeply influenced me in my early twenties, introduced me to this paradox. He wrote, "Live life as if everything depended on you. Pray as if everything depended on God." For more than thirty years

I've been guided by this paradox, and I've wondered about it. Basically, in words from the well-known serenity prayer, it guides us to accept what must be accepted, change what can be changed, and seek the wisdom to know the difference.

Rich possibilities lie in paradox. When we ignore or deny part of life's paradox, we forfeit those possibilities. Our nation's founders, for example, based our democracy on respect for life as it appears in diverse faiths and ideas, on compromise, and on service of the future. Now, however, more and more politicians ignore this heritage; they use oppositional tactics; they govern with an either/or, win/lose mentality in which those with the most power win. Many excellent leaders are recognizing this shift and are leaving the political arena in disgust or despair. Democracy is diminished when we become imperious about our own ideas and fail to accept life as it presents itself in others.

Guides for balancing the poles of the paradox

How do we live in the paradox? How do we bow to life as it is and change life at the same time? Here are some reminders I've found helpful:

1. Know the distinction between hope and expectation. With hope, we can hold the possibility that what is may be different; at the same time, we can avoid the expectation that it *must* be different. Rather than setting up opposition between the present and the future with our expectations, we can live in the fullness of hope.
2. Recognize opposition when you are in its presence. Recognize when you are *pushing* the river of life, not *flowing* with it. For example, when you sense an argument starting in which *either* you *or* the other must win, stop; take a breath; and let yourself be in unknowing about what's best in the situation. While in unknowing, consider the big picture, allowing time for new possibilities to emerge. Do you see a way you both can win?
3. If you find yourself in opposition to what is, bow to it. Do not attempt any service or any change until you have fully accepted the reality of the situation.

4. Before taking action, breathe deeply as you observe and accept exactly what is. Observe endlessly for new openings.
5. Always consider the big picture. In every situation be sure that you honor the ancestors—the parents and the parents' parents; and be sure that your action will serve the future—the children and the children's children.

Living fully may simply be the act of balancing two sides of what seems a paradox, of balancing effort and effortlessness, being and doing, action and inaction, giving and receiving.

When we hold the paradox of life, when we serve life while also accepting life as it is, then a peacefulness comes. Then we can live fully, even joyously, in the presence of what might be viewed as opposition.

Spring 1996

Healing for the Sake of Everyone

THE CHIEF EXECUTIVE OF A CORPORATION in a highly competitive industry in Washington State is an acupuncture patient and a student in the Institute's SOPHIA program (School of Philosophy and Healing in Action). Recently he told me about a meeting, crucial to the future of his company, where he dared to start the meeting by asking the eight executives gathered around the table to spend a half hour reading a list of the company's employees, more than a hundred names, and to add whatever they knew about each employee's family—children, grandparents, spouses.

At the end of the exercise, an accountant-type at the table added up all the names mentioned and reported that at least 648 people would be affected by the decisions made at the meeting. My patient said that throughout the day, if the meeting got into a difficult space—the space between small-minded, short-term solutions and bigger-minded, longer-term solutions—then someone at the table would mention one of the grandchildren and say, "What should we do for her sake?"

One of the teachings in the SOPHIA program is that we consider making our decisions in a way that honors our parents' parents and serves our children's children. This is a native American tradition and also a way taught in most of the world's ancient traditions. It is refreshing to take this wider perspective on the decisions and actions we craft each day, especially in our culture so dominated by advertising and actions based on impulse, moods and emotions, and where we so often hear the phrase, "I did it because I felt like it." Ancient cultures had little choice. Because survival was at stake, everyone was aware of the importance of service to each other.

I once treated a woman troubled with repeated headaches who worked in a very creative, highly stressful position. Acupuncture helped alleviate her pain and helped her continue to function in difficult circumstances. Yet she delayed making shifts in her lifestyle that would remove sources of her distress.

One day the woman's dog got sick. She took the dog to a wise veterinarian who at first glance thought the dog was being abused.

After he talked to her for a while, however, the veterinarian realized that when the woman was sick, the dog stayed very close to her, and, it seemed, absorbed some of the pain of the headache. When the veterinarian hinted that the woman's headache might be the source of her pet's pain, she made those long-delayed lifestyle changes. She never again had a headache.

Over the years I have asked many patients, "If you were feeling better, whom would it serve?" Often the question is a shock. Folks realize that for the sake of others they are willing to make changes they would not make for their own sake. So I offer my patients this possibility: When considering our personal well-being, our relationships with friends and relatives, our work in a business or corporation—at the moment of decision, the appropriate question might not be "What do I feel like doing?" or "What would make me happy?" It may be that genuine happiness comes from asking other questions: "What action in this moment will honor my parents' parents—all of the generations that have gone before?" And equally important, "What action would best serve not only my children, but their children and their children's children, so that I act in the biggest mind possible?"

I remember a young practitioner in a study group years ago asking, "What would happen if I took seriously the concept of the Tao—of Oneness—in the treatment room?" She paused, thinking, and then spoke as if suddenly enlightened: "It would mean that I wouldn't see the patient and me as separate, but as part of the Oneness. And I'd see us there for the sake of *everyone*—for the Oneness."

My promise to my patients is that as I treat them I will call them to the biggest possible mind, to the biggest possible vision of service. Over the 25 years of my practice, I've found that pain and suffering held in the context of service is vastly different from pain and suffering held as a personal problem.

That is also the promise of Tai Sophia Institute—to call all who study here to a larger vision of life, and in so doing call other institutions to the service of future generations.

Summer 1997

We are Kosovo, We are Littleton — We are One

AS I WRITE, OUR NATION is in the midst of a conflict in Kosovo. We are in opposition. Us versus Them. The people of one tradition versus people of another tradition, of one language versus those of another. Eight years ago, on the eve of the day of the start of the Gulf War, I remember hearing Thich Nhat Hanh speak as U. S. planes were flying over Iraq, dropping their bombs. Before a hushed crowd of 1600 people, this gentle teacher said that *he* was the American pilot, *he* was Saddam Hussein, *he* was the Iraqi soldier, and President Bush. He owned in his own body personal accountability for all that was happening. He did not place blame. He accepted his oneness with all of humanity.

At that moment I felt something was changing in American culture, for that well-dressed, well-educated audience was listening with deep respect to what seemed a radically new view of conflict and self and community. Yet Hanh's teaching of oneness is almost as old as humanity. The texts of the many traditions—the Judeo-Christian, Islamic, Hindu, Buddhist, Native American, Taoist—all point to life as a oneness in which we are all accountable for one another.

I remember the words of a Tai Sophia graduate who often treated inner city clients at the Sign of Jonah clinic in Washington, D.C. At a meeting of the clinic's staff, she said, "One day I was thinking about what would happen if I took the Tao seriously in the treatment room. I realized that I wouldn't see my patient and me as separate. Instead," she said, "I'd see us as the oneness *appearing* as two. And we would work together to discover how we could become whole, how we could better serve all of our family and friends, our community and the entire planet."

Wonderful possibilities emerge as we begin to see the oneness. Most of the time, though, we dwell in an illusion of separateness. After the Littleton massacre, I saw a young woman, a Littleton high school student, interviewed on TV. When asked her opinion about why the tragedy happened, she said (and I paraphrase): "I don't want to excuse those boys for what they did—that was wrong. But the rest of us were wrong, too. We made fun of them all the time. In a way, we were attacking them. And I think this was their way of getting back at us. They were different, and the rest of us didn't try to get past that. No one ever taught us ways of being with each other that would help us get past the differences." At that point, the interviewer cut her off. He seemed uneasy that she wasn't following the usual formula and placing blame. It's generally accepted in our culture that we separate out who's wrong and who's right, who's bad and who's good. It's hard for us to imagine how we would behave in a world where we didn't place blame.

What would it mean if we began looking for how one action begat another action begat another action? In such a world, how would we view the guns and addictions in the inner city? Would we see them as a call to the oneness? What about the many people for whom heroin has become a best friend? Would their addictions cease as they found new ways to have friendship—as people reached out to them in the oneness?

At Tai Sophia we are working to bring relationship back to healing, to return oneness to treatment rooms and to our communities. We are developing ways of helping people like the young woman in Littleton "get past the differences." Our efforts include practical steps to evoke the oneness wherever we are—at school, at work, in our homes, in our communities—steps based on teachings such as these:

- Oneness means that we dwell for the sake of each other.
- No blame for the past. The present moment is the starting point

for all that is to come. Bow to what is.

- When you create aliveness in others, it shows up in you.
- In any decision, think of the seven generations: Does your action honor the parents of your parents' parents? Will it serve the children of your children's children?
- When we encounter opposition—when the One shows up as Two—remember that opposition signals a lack of understanding, that problems can become opportunities, that symptoms can teach us.

And always, always return to the largest possible view—to the oneness.

This poem by Thich Nhat Hanh wonderfully illustrates that largest view and presents to all of us another possibility for our lives.

Please Call Me by My True Names

Don't say that I will depart tomorrow—
even today I am still arriving.

Look deeply: every second I am arriving
to be a bud on a Spring branch,
to be a tiny bird, with still-fragile wings,
learning to sing in my new nest,
to be a caterpillar in the heart of a flower,
to be a jewel hiding itself in a stone.

I still arrive, in order to laugh and to cry,
to fear and to hope.
The rhythm of my heart is the birth and death
of all that is alive.

I am a mayfly metamorphosing
on the surface of the river.
And I am the bird
that swoops down to swallow the mayfly.

CONTINUED

I am a frog swimming happily
in the clear water of a pond.
And I am the grass-snake
that silently feeds itself on the frog.

I am the child in Uganda, all skin and bones,
my legs as thin as bamboo sticks.
And I am the arms merchant,
selling deadly weapons to Uganda.

I am the twelve-year-old girl,
refugee on a small boat,
who throws herself into the ocean
after being raped by a sea pirate.
And I am the pirate,
my heart not yet capable
of seeing and loving.

I am a member of the politburo,
with plenty of power in my hands.
And I am the man who has to pay
his "debt of blood" to my people
dying slowly in a forced-labor camp.
My joy is like Spring, so warm
it makes flowers bloom all over the Earth.
My pain is like a river of tears,
so vast it fills the four oceans.

Please call me by my true names,
so I can wake up
and the door of my heart could be left open,
the door of compassion.
—THICH NHAT HANH

This poem was written in 1978, during the time when Thich Nhat Hanh was helping the boat people who fled oppression in Indochina.

Reprinted from *Call Me By My True Names* (1999) by Thich Nhat Hanh, with permission of Parallax Press, Berkeley, California, www.parallax.org.

Honoring the Cycles—in Society and Our Personal Lives

SUMMERTIME DELIGHTS. Last evening, in a balmy and beautiful August twilight, I shared with friends an outdoor dinner of corn on the cob, fresh tomatoes and salmon. Living was light, the talk was wonderful—life in its glory.

As I write, many folks are off on vacation. I myself, later this week, will spend time in Glacier National Park, and next week, on San Francisco Bay. It will be a time of ease and lightness of being, of a sense of wellness, of truly being blessed.

I think back to summertime in the city growing up and the trips to Rockaway Beach and the hanging-out time with family. I think of the glorious times together in the rhythm of the winter solstice holidays of Christmas, New Year, Hanukkah, Kwanzaa. I think of the enormous rush home across America every year at Thanksgiving, when people take time to be with their friends and relatives; and I remember the joy of the fireworks in the summer on the Fourth of July. Seldom do we appreciate or even understand the significance of these cyclical rituals for human life.

I read recently that aboriginal cultures spend about three hours a day in work to provide all the necessities of food and shelter, and that the rest of the time is devoted to rituals and holidays, feasts and travels. So our rituals of holidays, of summertime vacations, of travel, of returning to nature—these are remnants of a rhythm of life that centered around rest and time together, honoring and enjoying our human connection. These rituals provide certain defined, acceptable times when we take a break from the relentless modern culture of work.

I am aware that our public holidays often honor some special event. I wonder what would result if we spoke of these special days not simply as times of observance, but also as times reserved for resting, for being together, for enjoying the quality of being? I wonder if the level of violence in our society would decline if we used holidays—consciously—to care for each other and rebuild our sense of community.

Also on this summertime morning, I am aware of many young

people preparing to go off to college or to kindergarten—the annual return-to-school part of the yearly cycle. We send these children to prepare for what? To be whatever you want to be, we tell them. To get to know who you are. To become (fill in the blank). In these days we hear many voices wondering about our teenagers and their values, about increasing drug use and violence. Yet I doubt that we would hear many of these voices, or the young people themselves, saying that they go to school for the sake of making the world a better place for their grandchildren. I doubt that the question of responsibility for future generations has even been raised for many of them.

That we leave the world a better place for our grandchildren is often the rhetoric of political rallies on our holidays. Yet it is not a part of school application forms or catalogs, nor is it on the minds of parents as they send children off to school. If we have an intention for schooling, it's to help us live a better life, to earn more money, to be comfortable, to do what we want to do. Rarely do our intentions reflect the ancient wisdom of the Native American tradition, in which the ultimate purpose of any endeavor is to honor the ancestors and serve the grandchildren. In this view, each of us is part of the great cycle of life from ancient times into the future.

I wonder what would occur if we spoke of schooling not so much as a personal, individual "leg up" in the world, but rather as something undertaken "for the sake of the grandchildren." What if our society, from the moment our children turned 13 or 14, imbued them with responsibility for the next generations?

I wonder, too, what would happen if our grade schools based their curricula on an awareness of the fundamental cycles of nature. Many agree that something is missing in our educational system, something we might call spirit or meaning. This "something" that shows up as missing fuels the great debate about the role of religion in our schools, as well as discussion about how all the great world traditions, religions and philosophies will come together in our modern American world. (*Educational Leadership,* December 1998/ January 1999, devotes the entire issue to a discussion of spirituality and education.)

Consider, however, what the simple observing of nature could bring to our schools and our lives. Consider how our lives would be nourished by paying attention to what brings us delight in the summer holidays, in our evenings eating together, in the feasts of Thanksgiving and our winter celebrations. What would happen if as a nation we paid attention to the embodied response we all have to shifts in nature, to the rituals of holidays, to the value of time off as well as activity, to observing the laws of nature and recovering a lightness of being?

As I write, Maryland is experiencing a drought. Suddenly we are conscious that rain doesn't always fall, that it is subject to great and complex cycles of heat and cold in the ocean, air, and earth. At the moment, the cycle has brought us dryness, and suddenly we must prepare for that. I've noticed that public officials have not spoken about all of us gathering together to tend each other through this difficult time. Rather, they speak about punishing individuals who water their lawns and otherwise fail to observe restrictions. The expectation is that people will report their neighbors' violations and then police will tell these neighbors that they shouldn't be watering their lawns; it isn't assumed that one neighbor should speak to another with a sense of common purpose.

You might say that no matter how the neighbors handle it, the end will be the same—water will be conserved. Yet, the end *won't* be the same. One way brings us together, the other divides.

How we attend to such matters makes a difference in our communal and personal lives. The way of radical individualism cuts us off from each other and a shared sense of nature's cycles. The other way—the way of caring community—gathers us to support each other in learning to dwell wisely with the forces of nature.

In a society pervaded by a radical individualism, people tend to view their lives in terms of individual success and failure. We have little awareness of how totally dependent we are on each other—for water, for food, for travel, for mail, for telephones and e-mail, for comfort. And rarely do we appreciate the cycles of relationship—parents, children, grandchildren, friends—and the cycles of celebration we share. As we become more conscious of our relationships and shared experience, we may discover that these are the heart of a meaningful and successful transit between our birth and our death.

Speaking at the recent Noetic Sciences conference in Florida, Orem Lyons, a representative of one of the great councils of Native Americans, pointed out that the cycles of nature are unmerciful. When summer is done and winter begins, you can't plead with nature to be merciful and allow for a rerun of summer so you can prepare for winter. Nature moves in immutable cycles—cycles we sometimes fail to respect, to the detriment of our well-being.

Recently I've examined a number of individuals who have spent a great deal of money as they've gone through diagnostic tests and treatments for serious illnesses, and I've been struck by how many of them were not eating properly, getting very little sleep, and seldom going for walks or otherwise getting exercise. They expected their bodies to keep up with the pace at which they thought they should dwell, even while they violated cycles of night and day, of rest, of activity, of nurturance.

What if all of us supported each other in observing nature's cycles in our homes, the workplace, our communities? What if schools taught how to live well with the cycles from the earliest grades, and if the media reflected and encouraged this commonsense way to live our lives?

Life moves in the inevitable cycles of birth and death, of joy and sadness, warmth and cold. We must bear with each; we do not get a choice. The question is, do we—as individuals and as a society—have the wisdom to honor nature's cycles for the sake of the children and the children's children?

Ways to honor the cycles and care for all life ...

- Speak with each other often about our oneness—the oneness of the whole planet, including all races, cultures, religions, plants, animals—and search for ways to dwell in harmony with all that is. Remember: We are alone and lonely only when we forget that we are totally connected to all of life.

- Engage in a public discussion about our common need for rest, and for setting aside one day of the week especially for rest.

- Speak explicitly about the connection of our holidays to nature's cycles. Note, for example, how Thanksgiving celebrates the end of harvest, how so many of our religious holidays cluster around changes in the movement of the sun—the winter solstice (Christmas, Hanukkah, Kwanzaa) and the vernal equinox (Passover and Easter). Acknowledging that our diverse holidays have common roots in nature helps us recognize our oneness.

- Speak often about honoring the ancestors and learning from them, of living our lives in a way that creates a better world for the children's children. At the beginning of each school year, ask the students: "What will you create this year that will serve your grandchildren as yet unborn?"

Autumn 1999

Awakening the Inner Healer

"IS IT THE NEEDLE, THE HERB? What is it that's creating the change?" This is the question we hear from people conducting research on the outcomes of Tai Sophia's work in our Penn North Neighborhood clinic in inner city Baltimore. The answer to that question: The *individual* is creating the change.

The needle or herb or yoga or t'ai chi—these are the fulcrums around which change can occur if the individual chooses to take on life practices that create movement, that heal, that sustain well-being. Our research on the outcomes of acupuncture shows that satisfied patients are those who have taken on lifestyle practices that enable them to use their symptoms—their asthma, back pain, addiction—as teachers about how to stay well. Acupuncture has been the mechanism that facilitated that change, the tool that awakened them to their inner healing potential.

I'm reminded of the well educated, financially successful business executive who came for acupuncture treatment. At our first meeting, she handed me a stack of medical reports and tests costing almost $100,000. As we sat and talked together—it was two o'clock in the afternoon—I asked her, "What have you eaten today?" "A cup of coffee," she said.

"What did you eat last night?" "A hamburger."

"And water—how much do you drink in a day?" "A glass or two, plus sodas."

"What time did you go to bed?" "After midnight."

"What time did you get up?" "A little after five o'clock."

"When did you last get some exercise?" "Went for a walk about three weeks ago."

"Do the symptoms ever go away?" "You know," she said, "they were much, much better when I went on vacation with my friend."

I summarized for her: "So you tell me that you don't eat properly, you don't drink enough water, don't get enough sleep and very little exercise. And you also say that your symptoms clear up when you go on vacation. You're here in this office to find a cure. You've been looking to a hundred thousand dollars worth of tests to give you a clue about how to get well—and your body is telling you all the time!

"Needles can help you make the change," I told her. "They can be the catalyst, awaken the possibility for you. Yet the reality is that you must recover the art of eating and sleeping and breathing and getting exercise."

She paid attention. Assisted by acupuncture's needles and her practitioner's encouragement, this woman began to replace her hurtful old habits with simple, healthful practices.

All of the world's great healing traditions have taught simple practices that help people attain well-being in bodymindspirit. Here are a few:

• When you wake up in the morning, do you create a positive mood, what I call a "mood of creation"? Do the bumper stickers on your car echo that positive mood, or are you dwelling in complaint and upset? The mood that you create in the morning is contagious: it's picked up by others and fed back to you throughout the day.

• Do you live this day as though it were your last? If you knew that on this day you would breathe in and out for the last time, what would you do?

• Do you tend and build relationships? Do you keep things clear with your friends and loved ones? If you have a complaint or a squawk or an upset, do you immediately take clear, effective action—either make simple requests that will help clear the matter or completely let it go? Or do you hang on to bad feelings, dwell in them, cxplode?

• Do you live with common sense? For example, do you get enough rest? Do you breathe deeply? When you get upset and your breathing becomes shallow, do you notice and take a deep breath?

• Do you move your body enough? Stretch? Exercise? Do you drink plenty of water? Do you stay away from (or keep to a minimum) the sweet and caffeinated drinks so many people use to keep them going? Do you eat simple foods that nourish you? Do you pay attention to what your body (not just your mind) tells you about what you eat and drink?

This fall, the Institute expands to include Master's programs in Botanical Healing and in the Applied Healing Arts (we like to call it the AHA! program), along with our 25-year-old Master's in Traditional Acupuncture. Yet we are not shifting the focus of what we do at Tai Sophia. With these programs we make more explicit what has always been implicit in our work: acupuncture or any healing technique is the means through which individuals reawaken the possibilities within themselves. This reawakening requires more than the needles, the herbs, or any technique—it demands partnership between practitioner and patient, a set of practices for vibrant well-being, and ways of caring for each other and nurturing the life we all share.

Spring 2001

“Fuzz” and the Art of Living

WHATEVER WE DO ON OUR BRIEF PASSAGE through life—whether we call it work or play, eating or sleeping—is simply our attempt to move through life as smoothly as we can. We tend each other, knowing instinctively that such tending gives our lives stability, that it holds life together. Yet so often we falter and disrupt our lives—we haven’t mastered the art of living.

The world-famous physicist Hans Peter Dürr, the Heisenberg Professor of Physics at the Max Planck Institute in Munich, often uses a ball of string to illustrate concepts in quantum physics. He pulls the ball out of his pocket, tosses it up and down, unravels it, and asks folks what they see. “Well, it’s pretty simple,” they’ll say. “You can unwind the ball into a long thread and measure it.” Then he rolls the thread into a ball again and tosses it in the air. “What holds it together?” he asks. People observe that the whole is held together by tiny bits of fuzz along the thread. No fuzz, no ball. “The fuzz,” he says, “is life’s love. It holds life together.”

It’s so easy to ignore life’s “fuzz.” Even scientific trials will control for or eliminate the “fuzz” that is fundamental to life. And yet, it’s the fuzz, the love—something that happens in our everyday interactions—that holds life together. Here’s another analogy:

A ship on the ocean must always keep its bow headed into the waves. When the ship goes sideways to the waves, it will start to rock and eventually capsize if the waves get too strong—the ship gets its stability from it's direction. As we human beings navigate between birth and death, we stay steady by directing ourselves toward love. Love is our stability.

Everywhere there's evidence about the importance of life's "fuzz," life's intangibles. We hear many reports about the elderly who, though very ill, cling to life until they have completed a piece of work. This can be as simple as getting to the next birthday, the next New Year, or, recently, to the new millennium. It can be the resolution of a relationship, saying good-bye to a distant loved one, or completing a cherished project. Purpose, relationship, and love keep showing up as key ingredients in the continuum from birth to death.

We often read and speak about relationship-centered healing. Perhaps the most frequent complaint of consumers of health care is "Nobody talks to me. Nobody listens to me. There wasn't time for a relationship." Relationship, we're told, is at the center of healing. We could turn that around, however. We could say it's the absence of relationship and purpose and love that's at the center of illness.

Years ago, I heard the noted scientist Candace Pert remark that our ability to separate mind, body, and spirit was a result of Descartes's giving the mind and spirit to the Pope so that science could have the body, and have it unencumbered by the rule of the church. Perhaps that is why the modern world speaks of the body, mind, spirit, and emotions as separate realities. Yet our day-to-day experience—and, increasingly, scientific evidence—tells us that our spirit affects our body, and that the well-being of our body affects our spirit and emotions. Personally, I no longer use those distinctions. I find it more helpful to think in terms of a continuum of density: I think of my "humanbeingness" as expressed all the way from the heavy density of my bones to my thoughts—that least-dense aspect of one's self, which, without any physicality, can touch another.

What does this imply for the work we do at Tai Sophia Institute? It suggests that the art of healing, the art of living well between birth and death, may be as simple as learning the art of friendship, the art of conversation, the art of honoring the ancestors and of tending the next generation. It reminds us that all we are doing between birth and death is tending each other, holding together with love. We are holding each other straight into the waves of life, facing them together and with purpose, facing them for the sake of the next generation.

Our task is to learn those arts of healing—the art of speaking and listening, the art of tending each other, the art of the meal, the art of the walk, the art of life's dance.

As an academic institution, Tai Sophia has the exciting task of recovering the healing arts and the simplicity of life from ancient wisdom. Thus, we bring together wonderful scholars who question the certitudes of modern culture and explore alternatives—thinkers like Hans Peter Dürr, who, with a fuzzy ball of yarn, illustrates what holds all life together, and Ivan Illich, who points out that death is part of the cycle of life, and that what life is really about is deep friendship, *amicitia.*

The Institute must recover the simplicity of life, the simple arts of living and healing, and find a language for speaking about that simplicity. As we teach specific skills, we must embed them in this deeper wisdom. And at all times, we must remember that Tai Sophia is not an "institution." Tai Sophia is a gathering place where people share life, learning from each other and caring for each other on the passage between birth and death.

Summer 2001

How Can We Live Well in Unknowing?

IT WAS A BEAUTIFUL LABOR DAY weekend. Susan and I drove to a delightful restaurant in Baltimore's Little Italy for dinner with her cousin Patti and family. They met us there on their way back to New York after several days vacationing at Rehoboth Beach. We enjoyed a long, sumptuous meal. The talk was delicious. Mark, Patti's husband, told us about their vacation. Never before had he felt so close to his family, he said. Never had he had such a wonderful time with his children.

This committed man went on to tell us about his work and his dreams. I remember listening almost in disbelief as he described his daily three-hour round-trip commute from outer Long Island to the World Trade Center in lower Manhattan. The trip was worth it, he felt. It took him to a job that allowed him to support his family and educate his children.

After treatment-planning class on September 11, as I walked out of classroom 3, someone told me that a plane had crashed into the World Trade Center. Immediately I thought of Mark, of our conversation, of the delight we had all shared just a few days before. With tears in my eyes I thought about Patti and wondered what had happened to Mark. That morning, as Tai Sophia students and faculty gathered for meditation and prayer, and as Sherman Cohn led Kaddish, I wondered. Later that day I called Patti. No one knew anything.

We were in the middle of mystery, of unknowing. How to bear it? In the midst of the unknowing, I remembered something taught me by my fourth grade teacher, Sister Jean Marie—something for which I'm very grateful, and something I did not truly understand for many years. Almost every day she would say to us fourth-graders, "Now remember, when you go to bed tonight, be sure you are at peace with everyone. Is there anything you need to say? Make it clear to people that you love them, because some of them may not be around tomorrow." What wisdom!

In October, Susan and I flew to Long Island for a memorial service. As we boarded the plane we were in unknowing about so many things—about our flight, for one. For another, we were in unknowing about what we would find when we arrived. Would folks be craving revenge, seeking justice, or simply be present to the mystery of life?

Hundreds attended the service. These people from many faiths reached out to each other with smiles when the priest said it was the first time he had celebrated a memorial mass for a "good Jewish boy." We were struck that no one spoke of anger or revenge. And we were struck by the sense of oneness—the sense of individuals deeply caring for each other, wide awake to family and to the preciousness of the moments that we have together; the sense of absolute commitment to taking care of each other; the sense that all we have is this moment and each other. And all around us was a sense of awe, a sense of the mystery of life.

Sitting at Patti's kitchen table after the memorial service, talking with a young couple, I realized that the man across the table was alive only because he had forgotten to set his alarm clock. He had started out late for work on September 11, never making it to the World Trade Center. In grief and unknowing, he wondered aloud why he was alive and 63 friends were gone. He had attended 22 memorial services in the past few weeks.

In the weeks after September 11, several political leaders in Maryland have told me that what has kept them steady through these days are the practices taught at the Institute. Tai Sophia, they said, is an enormous resource for our community. One of these leaders, Maryland State Legislator Liz Bobo, earlier this year wrote about her experience at Tai Sophia: "In my work-life I've needed to learn how to bow to life *as it is*—another of the basic SOPHIA principles. This is a big first step for me....I've been at countless meetings where someone sees an issue opposite from the way I do. Can I bow to that, rather than be in opposition? Can I create a moment where there is a seed planted for both of us to begin to work together?" What wisdom for the work we must do as a community, a nation, and a community of nations!

Like these political leaders, I too have learned at Tai Sophia the practices that keep me steady. For example, it's only through my work in the Institute and SOPHIA that I've taken on the practice of allowing myself to be in unknowing, in mystery, in awe; the practice of holding myself steady and not rushing to judgment or to action.

I realize that some of the practices most essential to healing are complements to our society's impulse to act quickly, often too quickly and harshly. By not skipping the "unknowing," the "winter" of the creative cycle, we avoid the rough edges of quick anger and the rage of revenge. As we listen deeply and wait, we begin to identify the skillful, often subtle actions required to create well-being for ourselves, our families and communities and all of humankind.

I'm very aware that although I have four graduate degrees, in many ways I continue to be illiterate about the subtle skills of living well in nature and in everyday life. Now, through the practice of acupuncture and the art of healing, I've begun to learn these skills. In times of unknowing, especially, I'm grateful for learnings such as these...

- *Power* builds through periods of deep silence and rest.
- Acute *clarity* and *vision* arise as we ponder, in true unknowing, all the possibilities.
- Breathing deeply, we transform fear into *courage.*
- Transforming revenge into thoughtful, effective action creates *justice.*
- Deep *security* comes only with acceptance that there *is* no security.

It is my commitment that Tai Sophia's School of Philosophy and Healing in Action will make a major contribution to the literacy of living, that through SOPHIA the generations to come can master the arts of living in what is essentially a world of mystery and unknowing.

Winter 2002

Common Sense
in the Healing Community

Can Acupuncture Help Gout?

RECENTLY I RECEIVED A PHONE CALL from a man with a very strong French accent. Referred by a friend, he asked me if acupuncture could help his gout. At the moment of his call, I had only a short time to speak to him, so I got directly to the point. I said, "I've never met gout walking around all by itself. It comes connected to a human being who has many other symptoms which are uniquely combined in that individual." And gout, I told him, whatever it is, shows up differently in that individual from day to day—some days more strongly, some days less so. To determine whether I might help him, I said that I would need to meet him and learn much more. His response: "Oh, thank God. You've not going to give me the usual American hype." I referred the man to a wonderful individual who practices acupuncture near where he lives.

That conversation was not unusual. Acupuncture practitioners and students are asked constantly if acupuncture can help a particular disease. When they have learned the art of responding to that question, they have acquired one of the keys to starting a healing relationship. The question involves two assumptions, usually unexamined, that are endemic in our mechanistic culture. The first assumption is that disease is an entity that lives apart from the individual—that "gout," for example, stands by itself, a thing apart from our total selves. The second assumption sees acupuncture as a technique, a disembodied tool used to "fix" a disease.

All great physicians, including William Osler, a founder of modern Western medicine at Johns Hopkins medical school, focus on the patient: it is the patient who receives treatment, not the disease, for the power to heal himself resides within that individual. Each person's unique discomfort is a messenger from the bodymindspirit calling the individual to the way home.

I think of the title of Dianne Connelly's book, *All Sickness Is Homesickness*. Society has taught us to see our symptoms as problems to be "fixed," rather than as signs that point us home—signs that point the way to healing.

Thus an acupuncture student is reminded repeatedly not to label a patient (nor allow patients to label themselves) with disease words: asthma, arthritis, fibromyalgia, chronic fatigue, or even the expressions that often appear in Oriental medicine such as "Rising Liver Fire" or "Water Causative Factor" or "stuck chi." These diagnostic nomenclatures may serve a limited purpose, but for the most part, they distract us from the unique signs given off by this unique individual on this particular day. And it is the uniqueness, the specificity, that enables individuals—often with the assistance of another—to find their way back to living as well and as fully as possible.

Who is this practitioner who assists another? Just as our culture views diseases as standardized things, it views practitioners as technicians delivering standardized treatments. Perhaps it would be more appropriate and helpful to speak of these assistants as "healers"—healers who may use acupuncture, who may use Prozac, who may use St. John's Wort, who may use a surgical scalpel, who may manipulate the body—healers who are aware of each patient's unique pattern and use their tools accordingly. Very different actions may result than when practitioners view themselves as experts who administer techniques to "fix" diseases. J. R. Worsley, in his first small book on acupuncture, pointed out that it is the task of the acupuncturist—the healer—to envision persons as they would be when whole and well in themselves. As a young student, I heard J. R.'s words as reminding practitioners to remind their patients of "home"—of what it would be like when they allowed themselves to recover their wholeness.

What healers often do while using their "tools"—the acupuncture needle or drug or pill or touch—is to remind patients that living fully depends on breathing deeply, getting enough sleep, eating well, walking and exercising the body, having an appropriate pace, having values that honor the ancestors and serve one's children. It is through the appropriate balance of these components, together with the extraordinary gift of the needle (or the drug, or the touch), that patients recover their own healing ability. The needle, or any therapy, is only one of many components of healing, and the healer must use these "tools" guided by the uniqueness of each patient.

Having practiced for 25 years, I am well aware of the extraordinary power of the insertion of a needle—I've seen it create dramatic change. I know very well how essential the needle and other therapies can be in moving forward the healing process. However, I fear that emphasizing the power of these techniques will obscure the fact that they are only one element of a much more complicated process—the awakening of an individual's own healing powers.

These days, as we speak more and more about "integrative" and "whole medicine," we must be careful: We must not think that "wholeness" or "integration" come simply from applying an assortment of techniques and therapies. Rather, we need to develop an "integrative medicine" that can blend various healing possibilities uniquely to serve the unique individual—the one who is the heart of the healing process. We must remember that it is the patient who knows his or her way home, and that the healer serves simply as guide and helper—not the creator of wellness.

Meridians helps all of us, patients as well as practitioners, to remember these things. It tells stories of ways people heal themselves and learn to live more fully—stories that guide us in serving each other, stories that guide us on our own healing journey when, inevitably, our own symptoms arise and we need to find our way home.

Summer/Late Summer 1998

Back—and Forward—to the Basics

I WRITE AS I RETURN FROM a week amid the magnificence of nature in Yellowstone, Glacier, and Grand Teton National Parks. A city-born human, I watched in wonder as grizzlies made their way so purposefully—how did they know where to go? I stood near a huge moose, awestruck that a creature with such enormous antlers could move gracefully through the thick forest—how did he manage? In the silence of backwood trails, experiencing the wisdom and awe of nature, I knew that I didn't know: "He who speaks doesn't know. He who knows doesn't speak." (Lao Tzu)

And as I walked amid these wonders of nature, I felt the pain of living in a modern world removed from the common sense so available to the grizzly and the moose. That common sense, perhaps, has been removed from our lives by our modern education.

The day before I left on this trip, I encountered our loss of nature's common sense during conversations in the treatment room. I listened to the stories of two individuals who had come for treatment for the first time. Both had numerous complaints and had undergone many medical tests. Both had seen practitioners of complementary medicine. In each case, the patient had not taken seriously some of the most obvious basics of wellness and healing, and the practitioners had not discussed these basics with the patient.

I found myself saying to each of them, "If you get so little sleep and and eat so irregularly, if you drink so little fluid during the day, if you do all that aerobic exercise without paying attention to the depth of your breathing, if you don't take time to play with your friends or take in acknowledgment for the good work that you do—then all those symptoms do make sense.

With six hours' sleep, no breakfast, no regular habit of fluid intake, and the shallow breathing that you display, then it's quite wonderful of your body to exhibit the symptoms and get your attention!"

We then spent time talking about the commonsense changes that would help them heal themselves.

These individuals had come asking if acupuncture could help. I told them that acupuncture, like all other healing techniques, whether mainstream or complementary, serves well only in the presence of common sense and the basics of healing.

I am saddened at this loss of common sense about health in our culture, a loss I feel in myself and observed in these two individuals. Each of these patients had experienced at least twenty years of formal education, yet never really learned the commonsense basics of good health—basics well known to our ancestors who lived before biomedicine's experts and miracle drugs.

These days, Americans increasingly return to healing traditions that preceded the breakthroughs of Western biomedicine. Traditions that evolved in China, for example, had great common sense: Healing, they taught, started with exercise, with good food, with attention to herbs, with massage and bodywork. Then, when something more technical was needed, practitioners would use acupuncture. The ancients understood that through acupuncture, they were supporting the person's own inner power of healing.

Support that helps us heal ourselves

Two stories from the Tai Sophia clinic illustrate how acupuncture and a practitioner's coaching, combined with good life practices, support healing:

In conversation with a patient, I noticed how this accomplished and respected professional dismissed acknowledgment of the good work he does: "Oh, no. It's okay. I enjoy doing it," he said. During our discussion he recognized his pattern of self-disparagement. And he realized that when he listens and takes in the acknowledgment of those whom he serves, he both gives *and* receives, completing an important human exchange that nourishes everyone. This simple learning has had far-reaching consequences for this individual.

In another recent example, when a patient received a diagnosis of advanced cancer, we assisted her through the process of chemotherapy and radiation. She has done very well. As she began to recover her strength, I asked her if there was anything incomplete in her life. She considered the question, then told me that the cancer was a reminder that she had not yet forgiven one of her parents. She knew that in releasing the old story of upset and anger, more of herself was available for healing.

The old suffering didn't cause the illness. Nevertheless, she had learned an important truth: that when we hang on to the past—bad or good—there is less of us available to the present.

As this patient began to let go of the past, to live more in the present and to forgive, she said that she knew she was healing herself.

Missing in medicine

Excellent healers in Western traditions have taken a similar approach, reminding us that healing requires attention to the basic rhythms of life, to the fundamental forces that support us—friendship and love and caring, good food and good sleep. Yet with the rise of biomedicine and its technical miracles, practitioners in many traditions have lost sight of this heart of health and healing.

In the center section of this issue of *Meridians*, physician Elliott Dacher movingly tells about his own journey to find what was missing in his life and his practice of medicine.* What he discovers about "presence" and soul in healing has implications for the whole of American medicine.

Our opportunity: restore soul and common sense to medicine

Last spring, in a presentation to medical professionals at Johns Hopkins University, Elliott shared some of his personal journey as he led his listeners through the history of Western medicine. At the end of the talk, one physician stood up with tears in his eyes. "I'm

64 years old and I've been practicing for 36 years," he said. "I wish I had heard this lecture in medical school."

This physician, who is an excellent practitioner of the valuable techniques of biomedicine, had not been taught about the "heart" of medicine in medical school. Elliott, in his lecture that day, explained that the "heart"—the personal approach of earlier times—faded with the rise of biomedicine in the late 19th and 20th centuries.

Now, using common sense and wisdom, we have the opportunity to reunite science and healing. We must create a new medicine that draws on the invaluable techniques of science and of the complementary traditions, while also honoring what lies at the core of healing and good health: caring relationships in which we help each other tend well the simple basics of life.

Autumn 1998

*Elliott S.Dacher, "At the Heart of the New Medicine." *Meridians,* Autumn 1998.

Diverse Practitioners Join at the Heart of Healing

AS I WALKED OUT THE DOOR from a recent meeting on managed care, someone turned to me and said, "Don't let them turn you into a health-care provider!" I knew what he meant. The strictures and systems of managed care threaten the heart of what we do—these systems threaten the heart of healing.

I have practiced traditional acupuncture for 27 years, and the longer I practice, the more I realize that what I practice first and foremost is not acupuncture; rather, it is the art of healing, the art of being with others in a way that helps them discover their power to heal themselves. The acupuncture needles and points and words have been the way I bring this healing service, my way of connecting with others. There are many healing arts.

As acupuncture has expanded and "professionalized," it has encountered the dangers that come with professionalization, including turf battles and arguments about what healing method is "best." Some of the most publicized professional battles have occurred in state legislatures. Two years ago, for example, there was a confrontation in the Maryland legislature over whether acupuncturists or veterinarians should practice acupuncture on animals. Happily, the issue was resolved: all agreed that individuals from both groups should practice, if properly trained.

Later, a key legislator asked me how, in the end, Maryland

acupuncturists and veterinarians had come to such an amicable resolution. "And how do you avoid turf fights with the medical doctors?" he asked. "You never let them get you into an oppositional battle." The answer goes back to the 1970s, when several of us opened one of Maryland's first acupuncture centers and encountered opposition from the medical community. Since then, it has been our policy to listen to the concerns of doctors, of veterinarians and others until we hear the heart of their concerns. When we listen long enough, we discover that at the heart of what they say are concerns shared by everyone involved in healing. There is no conflict between the core interest of acupuncturists and the core interest of good-hearted physicians, whatever their technique.

The future does not belong to turf-battling, to managed care, to insurance systems. The future, I believe, belongs to *healers*. Within 10 or 20 years, I believe that a variety of highly trained professionals will speak of themselves as healers—healers who happen to bring particular skills to the service of others. The role of healer will be primary in their view, and they will feel a bond with others who also serve as healers; only secondarily will they see themselves as practitioners of a specialty.

I understand that in the current atmosphere, many practitioners are afraid that they will lose their identity, their respect and their incomes if they work collaboratively. And I understand how easy it is for a patient to generalize about a whole specialty on the basis of a single bad or good experience. In the next decade, however, I believe that all of us, practitioners and patients alike, will shift our focus so that healing, collaborative healing, becomes the focus of a new medicine.

At the moment, all professional systems appear to be divided between those who focus on relationship-centered care and those who focus on technique—a false dichotomy, it is abundantly clear to me. We live in an amazing time, for modern communication has brought into view the healing arts of many great civilizations. It is now our task—and privilege—to bring them together, under an umbrella large enough to hold them all—a concept of medicine not centered on techniques, but around an outcome already experienced by many patients: the recovery of the ability to heal oneself and nurture one's own well-being.

There is much work to be done to tear down barriers among professional groups and practitioners of various traditions, to remove remnants of turf wars, and to rework or remove standards that do not serve and that block good service. This work will be done jointly by patients and by practitioners who, regardless of their technique, place healing at the heart of their practice.

Spring 1999

Recovering Our Senses, Recovering the Ability to Heal Ourselves

SELDOM HAVE I ALLOWED MYSELF a moment of discouragement such as the one I experienced in the last days of 1999. The phenomena preceding that moment initiated a "winter of unknowing," and it brought me a very powerful learning experience.

It was a Wednesday afternoon. I was seeing patients, one after the other, going from room to room. I saw four relatively new patients in a row, and in each room had a similar experience. I asked simply, "How are you? What's going on? Tell me about yourself." And each time I heard what I might call hearsay or a secondhand story. All these individuals are well educated, very successful, fluent with ideas and speech. Yet in each case they responded with a label they had been given by a doctor, a label they had made up for themselves, or a label from a friend: "I have arthritis." "I have bursitis." "I have migraines." "I have cluster headaches." And in each case, I found that it was virtually impossible for them to describe the symptoms as they *experienced* them, or give details of the moments and hours before the symptoms appeared. They did not have simple language for the way an ache or a pain appeared in their forehead, or the way their breathing moved, or what happened in their body. It was a disheartening moment to realize that they could tell me *ideas* about their own body, yet had little concrete ability or language to share the actual sensations they experienced moving through their hands, their feet, their torso, their head.

For years I've known that a main part of my work—and, I believe, a principal effect of acupuncture—is to enhance people's sensory awareness of their own life, thus enhancing their healing—and their joy. Yet over the years, as individuals watch medical shows on television, read about medicine, speak in abstractions with their doctors and friends, they've come to have less and less awareness of themselves, a state that seems more and more prevalent. Self-awareness is key to healing, and increasingly, individuals lack this starting point for their journey to health.

And there were other incidents that fed my discouragement:

When I was teaching a seminar last fall, a young acupuncture practitioner, a graduate of a very fine acupuncture school in the western United States, came up to me after the first session and said, "Why are you talking about the senses? What does awakening the senses have to do with the practice of acupuncture?" At first I thought she was joking with me—but she was serious. She had studied acupuncture as a body of information out of which treatment decisions were made, and she had not realized that to use this knowledge well, she needed to awaken her senses. Even her pulse-reading provided only limited perception of what was going on within the person—not the richly textured explanations available through the multifaceted pulses; nor was she aware of the nuances of voice or sounds or colors or emotions.

In another seminar—the two-week SOPHIA intensive that starts Tai Sophia's Master of Acupuncture program—again I encountered similar sensory numbness. A loving young mother typified what I experienced in the group of fifty students. When describing her young daughter she could give us stories and labels—"bright," "hyperactive," and "difficult," for example. Yet she struggled to describe the simple phenomena of her nine-year-old. It was as if those labels were plastered over her eyes: She could not say without detailed questioning that her daughter had shortness of breath when afraid, was reading books ahead of her school level, had many close friends, and was asking too many creative questions for her teachers. Her mother knew all of this, yet it had to be pulled to the surface.

In the classroom and the treatment room, I often do the work of demanding that beginning students and beginning patients take off labels and open their senses to the phenomena of their life experience. As I tear apart their language, they almost seem to feel I tear apart their flesh—their encapsulated ch'i—until something new and wondrous begins to emerge: a life fully lived.

It's said that Shakespeare used 25,000 words to describe life and that the average college-educated person today is limited to 10,000. I fear that our language is being reduced to plastic words and concepts, making it difficult for our patients to know their own embodied experience of life. And with less and less capacity to know themselves, they must more and more turn themselves over to medical experts.

I've learned that in the moment of discouragement arises the opportunity. These last months have helped us here at Tai Sophia become more precise about what the learning and the teaching of the Institute must be. Tai Sophia's mission is to enable all of us to learn the arts of living and of dying, based on ancient wisdom and the observing of nature. Now, we see that fundamental to this mission is the ability to speak truly about life's phenomena.

And so, from my "winter of unknowing" emerges clarity about the critical work ahead of us:

First, we must take on the very basic work of awakening our senses and recovering a language that simply describes what is before us. This work is important for our culture. In the absence of such a discourse, I believe we will be reduced to ironic, judgmental commentaries, to ungrounded abstractions about life, so wonderfully described in a recent book by Jedediah Purdy: *For Common Things; Irony, Trust, and Commitment in America Today*. The task is to reawaken our senses, and then, before we describe it in poetry, to learn to describe our experience in the simplest of language: Is it dry? Is it hot? Is it cold? Is it open? Is it closed?...

Second, we need to bring people together to learn from each other. I'm aware that the language individuals use to describe their experience to me is a language they develop alone, largely in front of a television set. A lot of what I do in the treatment room, one on one, can best be done in groups. I could greet folks and then help them learn from each other. They don't need me.

They need to hear the enfleshed experience of others in suffering and in pain and in the process of healing. I think of the healing temples of ancient Greece where people began the healing process by attending a Greek tragedy and then speaking about it with each other. How do we create group occasions for us to learn together, to realize that we are all on a path between birth and death that includes suffering?

Third, practitioners must use their senses to assist healing. I often say that the practitioner doesn't really know how to treat a patient, because each patient is unique. Experienced practitioners have learned to allow each patient to teach them the best way to treat that unique individual. This work cannot be done from a formula—from abstract "symptoms," to a theory about pattern, to placing needles based on a theory about the pattern. What we want to create is a different world of treatment. That means practitioners open their senses, observe when movement occurs, and then enhance that movement.

What I write in this column—although catalyzed by recent experiences—is something that has developed in my understanding over 25 years in conversation with my colleagues at TAI. We seek to recover a world virtually unknown in the modern West, a world neglected as our culture developed its great ability to analyze and take things apart. However, my colleagues and I here at the Institute have a vision:

• that we develop graduate programs through which individuals recover their senses—their ability to see, to hear, to taste, to feel and to smell nature, to be in the presence of life as it is lived, and to observe and enhance the way it moves;

• that we develop a campus where many folks spend time together, enriching that learning, and sharing it with people who do research and clinical work;

• and that we build new ways through which people recover awareness, and thus gain the ability to heal themselves, requiring much less intervention from medical experts.

Though the actual programs will have labels like "Acupuncture," "Applied Philosophy," "Nutrition" and "Herbology," sensory awareness will be at the heart of all.

So out of discouragement has arisen hope. And that hope is grounded, perhaps, in an understanding of the deepest root of the issue—that our senses are closed and that we must open them. And that comes around to something I've known for 25 years. Something for which I've never quite had the language and the clarity that I've gained through allowing myself the winter of unknowing.

And so I invite you to go into your own winter of unknowing, for out of that experience can come the hope of spring with its vision of what can be. Here at Tai Sophia that vision is of recovering our senses and thus our common sense, of regaining our own innate ability to heal ourselves and others.

Spring 2000

Dangers in the Mainstream

I OFTEN TELL OUR ACUPUNCTURE STUDENTS that I wish they were licensed by the Department of Parks and Recreation rather than the Department of Health. I say this to emphasize that what they are about is *wellness,* not illness, not pathologies and the fixing of diseases—the work of the Department of Health. Rather, the work of a graduate of this institute is helping folks to enjoy life, to live life fully, and to know their symptoms as teachers and guides—more like the Department of Parks and Recreation. As people's lives expand into wellness, the pathologies that brought them to acupuncture heal from the inside out.

In the world at large, however, the wisdom of ancient China's healing arts has been turned into a *system* that deals with Western-defined pathologies. The president of a major Chinese university expressed concern about this development when he visited Tai Sophia two years ago. And recently, I read three articles by distinguished acupuncture practitioners who are concerned with this same issue: They fear we may lose the richness of our tradition—the richness that comes from what the ancients taught about living life fully—as we strive to show we can deal with pathology more cheaply and effectively than Western medicine. There are two issues here about the nature of science: one is economic, the other is philosophic.

As the First Continental Congress of the United States debated and voted on freedom of religion and of speech, it also fiercely debated freedom of health care. This debate was led by physician Benjamin Rush, a signer of the Declaration of Independence who became the first surgeon general of the United States. Rush argued that the U. S. Constitution "should make a special provision for medical freedom as well as religious freedom." Without such a provision, he contended, scientists could become the new high priests, dictating a new orthodoxy. Two hundred years later, we can look back and see that Rush was wise. If we are not vigilant, a 21st-century scientific orthodoxy may endanger not only the public's freedom to choose from a full range of health care, but also the values at the core of our healing art.

Today I received an invitation to yet another conference on "integrated" medicine, where presenters will describe how research can support the integration of alternative medicine into the mainstream, and will promote reimbursement as part of that integration. Reimbursement is not necessarily a bad thing. Yet I wonder: At these meetings, are we keeping in mind the "heart" of healing? When I read about presentations to the White House Commission on Complementary and Alternative Medicine—presentations on questions such as "Is it evidence-based?" and "Should it be paid for by insurance?"—I hear the sound of a high-class "turf battle," a conversation based on the language and assumptions of modern mainstream medicine.

Having been involved for more than 30 years in another conversation, the conversation about wellness of body-mind-spirit, I'm aware of its deep and broad roots: It is born of many people creating a new way of thinking about themselves and their symptoms, and an old way of trusting the body's wisdom. That wisdom has spread, and folks have recovered ancient ways of healing and tending each other. Yet some unexamined assumptions have crept into the conversation (cherished and destructive assumptions, Ivan Illich would call them): It is assumed that alternative and complementary health care "should" be reimbursed by insurance, and that all we do "should" be certified by "gold standard" research evidence.

What goes unnoticed here? Have we asked whether double-blind research can address the essence of a healing art? And what about this mainstream system that many alternative practitioners seek to enter—how well has it served the community? How well do the economics of modern medicine work? Is this the way we really want to go? Unthinkingly, we are in danger of turning ourselves over to a system that ignores what is most important in our healing art.

At our Penn North Community Project in Baltimore's inner city, the Institute has demonstrated what can happen through our approach to healing, an approach rooted in ancient ways and wisdom. Without using the "system," Penn North has shown extraordinary results with people suffering from addiction and other ills. For example, a study funded by the Soros Foundation showed that arrest rates dropped significantly for persons who participated in the Penn North program. Such outcomes, made possible through the love and caring of the Penn North staff and the contributions of caring donors, are at least as good as mainstream system outcomes. All this has happened without reimbursement and at 25 percent of the cost of mainstream care.

Last year, Tai Sophia sponsored a gathering of distinguished scientists, who in their discussions took seriously Heisenberg's uncertainty principle and its implication that there is no truly objective observer, even in a scientific investigation. Objective research—the scientific "gold standard"—cannot be pure: the researcher is inescapably involved. Simply by observing, he changes what happens. This conversation about science, a core focus for the Institute, continues at our 2001 symposium. Tai Sophia must be part of a reexamination of science and its role in the healing arts.

As we start new programs in applied healing arts and botanical healing, and as we continue the immensely successful master's degree program in acupuncture, we have new opportunities and take up new challenges—challenges that really relate to a school of public health. We have the opportunity to show that the work we do serves in simple and powerful ways, bringing people into community, creating love, helping people care for themselves and others, and saving costs. And we have the challenge of examining the assumption that research, as presently applied, addresses what is crucial in the art of healing.

Through the work we are doing, how do we rediscover "science"? How do we reinvent and recover it as simply the observing of nature? How do we be of service to larger communities? This institute is committed to the delivery of service and to delivering it in a simple way that enriches people's lives; it is deeply committed to educating all of us so we are less dependent upon experts and more awake to our own senses, more knowing of our own ability to heal ourselves. In this way our work truly becomes part of the art of living well, not a system for dealing with pathologies and problems.

As I move into my sixties and listen to the national debates about Medicare, I'm very aware that there is no way to fund health care for my elder years unless we have the courage to recover the joy and excitement of living life well and fully. We need health care that helps us stay alive to our senses, helps us learn from our body's symptoms, and helps us tend ourselves as did the generations long before the advent of modern evidence-based trials and modern insurance systems.

Autumn 2001

Insurance Can't Assure What's Most Important

WHEN I WAS A CHILD, we rarely visited a doctor. I don't recall our family having any insurance. A local pharmacist provided much of the health care in our community, and often he was a friend of the family. Families knew remedies. We took care of each other in time of illness; we took each other in. Insurance in those days—the 1940s—would have been a formal guarantee of what was already guaranteed by our community: when ill, you would be cared for. In those pre-penicillin days, there was no thought of a guaranteed medical "fix."

Now, a short 50 years later, we think of insurance as paying for a technique. We ask, "Does insurance cover my surgery, my x-ray, my acupuncture, my herbal consultation?" And I ask, "Since insurance has become the norm, is our quality of life enriched?"

Although insurance may cover some necessary medical expenses, helping to protect us from life's scariness and unpredictability, it can't erase the fact that life includes pain and fright. Nor does insurance assist relationships—certainly not our relationship with our health-care providers; nor does it encourage supportive relationships within the community. The practice of "community," I believe, has disappeared from the conversation about health care, and the caring community has been undermined by impersonal insurance.

Since we have moved to our wonderful new building and campus, I've been surprised at how often visitors have said to me, "Now that you're 'mainstream,' when is insurance going to cover acupuncture and herbs?" I'm unsure how to answer. It's my instinct to say, "Frankly, we don't want insurance coverage because it could destroy the essence of how we serve." (And of course, those who know me know I'm aware that insurance is essential for many individuals and families.)

In this column I share my concerns about insurance. Perhaps these thoughts will ignite your own thinking and initiate a conversation that moves us toward a solution of our nation's health-care dilemma.

A few weeks ago I was surprised to see an article about placebo in the *Baltimore Sun*. It reported a controlled clinical trial showing that a sugar pill frequently was as effective as drugs such as Prozac or Zoloft. And the article noted another interesting phenomenon: individuals in this study often received hours of personal attention, raising the possibility that *attention* was the active ingredient.

Insurance encourages us to think of healing in terms of access to experts and their technologies. Yet research studies underscore what we know intuitively: consultation with experts is just one aspect of the healing process. Tai Sophia's research (including Claire Cassidy's studies of patients in six clinics in five states, and the Center for Social Research study of our Penn North clinic), as well as much of the research conducted by the National Institutes of Health, indicate that healing does not necessarily depend on access to experts and technologies. Rather, the roots of the healing response lie in the healing relationship and in the ability of individuals and families to take charge of their own health.*

I recall a woman, a patient of one of our graduates, who spoke to a class of medical students at Johns Hopkins last year. She had been seriously ill with five different major disease processes. Unable to walk and move about, confined to her home, she had been forced to retire. She acknowledged that she was tended by the heads of various medical departments at Hopkins. "I have had the best of medical care," she told the students. "But I didn't start to heal—*I didn't start to heal myself*—until I started acupuncture with Laura. Now, as you can see, I'm moving about. I am much happier. I still need the experts to tend my medications, although I take fewer and fewer meds. Now, at last, I've begun my healing." This woman's experience is beyond what insurance is currently designed to cover.

We are told that health-care costs will double in the next ten years. That means your health insurance premiums will double, whether you or your employer pays them. We are caught in what the health-care community terms the "iron triangle" conundrum: When we increase quality and access, we increase costs—and that's not acceptable. If we reduce costs, we must either reduce quality or reduce access—also not acceptable. Seldom do we question the basic assumption that health care is about access to experts and technologies. What if health care at its root is about personal responsibility and community—about how we take care of ourselves and each other? What would that new assumption imply for insurance and for how we interact with the health-care system, interact with our families and communities, with our doctors?

In 1975, when we opened the acupuncture clinic in Columbia, a local physician invited us to speak to his colleagues. At the conclusion of the meeting he said, "I'm highly trained to deal with pathology. But the day *before* a painful tummy becomes a pathology—when it's only a symptom—I can't do anything. I have to wait until it becomes an ulcer. If you know how to deal with the symptom before it becomes a pathology, maybe you can make a major contribution." This physician was pointing to the heart of health care and to what is missing in our system: the art of caring for ourselves and for each other. As we teach that art and practice it in our day-to-day lives, fewer and fewer symptoms move into pathology.

Before earning her acupuncture degree, one of our faculty members was a human resources director for a corporation. While there, she used some minor funding adjustments to encourage the corporation to experiment with what I call "watercooler medicine": In conversations (some of them at lunchtime gatherings arranged by the human resources department), individuals passed on to each other what they had learned about taking care of a health issue in a "natural" way.

Although this experiment was not formally documented, it appeared to succeed beyond expectation. Employees required fewer major medical interventions, reducing corporate health-care costs by almost 20 percent. The "watercooler" experiment stimulated community, sharing, caring for each other, early intervention, lifestyle change, prevention—all aspects of effective health care. I invite our readers to introduce "watercooler medicine" in their own family and workplace.

Perhaps the "iron triangle" can be broken. By returning to community we can provide appropriate low-tech and high-tech health care—including acupuncture and other forms of natural care—to the poor. For the most part, only the more affluent in our society have enjoyed the benefits of complementary care. Tai Sophia has initiated projects to bring these benefits to people in need, including individuals who are incarcerated and those struggling with addiction. *Creating community* and *encouraging self-care and care of others* are central to these projects.

The way out of the "iron triangle" (which is also what folks love about the work of the Institute) is to empower individuals and families and communities to take care of themselves, enabling them to pass on ancient wisdom about the art of living and dying from generation to generation. As we embody and pass on this knowledge, we will recover and sustain community. Then insurance will retake its appropriate place—a resource maintained by a caring community, so that in times of catastrophic need, members of the community have the ability to tend one another.

Summer 2002

* For reports on research conducted by Claire Cassidy, PhD, see *Meridians* Summer 1997 and Spring 1996. For a report on research conducted by the Center for Social Research at the Penn North clinic, *see Meridians* Summer 2001.

ABOUT TAI SOPHIA INSTITUTE:
A private, nonprofit, educational organization, Tai Sophia Institute is the anchoring academic institution for the nation's emerging wellness system. Founded in 1974, the Institute offers master's degree programs in Acupuncture, Botanical Healing, and Applied Healing Arts, as well as programs, workshops, and resources for the general public. For information about Tai Sophia, call (410) 888-9048 or visit the Institute's website: www.tai.edu.

PUBLICATIONS FROM TAI SOPHIA PRESS:

Traditional Acupuncture: The Law of the Five Elements
by Dianne M. Connelly

All Sickness is Home Sickness
by Dianne M.Connelly

To Come to Life More Fully: An East West Journey
by John G. Sullivan

Survey of Traditional Chinese Medicine
by Claude Larre, Jean Schatz, Elisabeth Rochat de la Vallée
Translation by Sarah E. Stang

Alive and Awake: Wisdom for Kids
by Dianne M. Connelly and Katherine Hancock

Books are available through the Meeting Point Bookstore, Tai Sophia Institute, 7750 Montpelier Road, Laurel, MD 20723, (410) 888-9048 ext. 6632.

For information about past issues of *Meridians,* contact the Meeting Point Bookstore or visit www.tai.edu.